The Thirteen Great
Economic/Business
Myths
That Dominate Our Lives

The Thirteen Great Economic/Business Myths That Dominate Our Lives

Sanford W. Kahn
Business Author & Speaker

iUniverse, Inc.
New York Lincoln Shanghai

The Thirteen Great Economic/Business Myths That Dominate Our Lives

iUniverse books may be ordered through booksellers or by contacting:

iUniverse
2021 Pine Lake Road, Suite 100
Lincoln, NE 68512
www.iuniverse.com
1-800-Authors (1-800-288-4677)

ISBN: 978-0-595-43983-6 (pbk)

ISBN: 978-0-595-88304-2 (ebk)

Printed in the United States of America

This book is dedicated to the

firm belief that....

"A secure future lies in economic growth."

Sanford Kahn
March, 2007

Contents

Myth #1:

Economics Is a Science

This myth is pure nonsense!

Since most people have very little to no understanding of how and what drives the economy, they assume that economics is an arcane science understandable only by the pundits. With our twenty-four hour news channels, this would be interpreted as the talking heads on TV.

When you hear the phrase such as the "laws of economics" it sounds vaguely similar to the scientific phrases like the "laws of physics" or the "laws of chemistry". Hence, people incorrectly associate economics with science.

Economics is…. the study of human behavior in its historical setting. The study of human behavior, if anything, is a branch of psychology not science. The first of the modern economists (Adam Smith for example) were philosophers who had an appreciation of human behavior. To carry this argument to its conclusion, the psychology departments in our colleges should be incorporated into the economics departments. But, this is an argument for another day.

To various degrees, most people have an interest in the how's and why's of human behavior. Therefore, as a reader of this book, you have graduated to being an honorary economist. Your views and opinions have the same weight as those expressed in the media.

The "myths" that follow are based on this central definition of economics.

Myth #2:

We live and work in an economy that is changing very rapidly.

One of the more popular and often repeated business and societal themes is that we live and work in an economy that is changing quickly. This is especially true with individuals who make their living selling programs or seminars dealing and adjusting to rapid and turbulent change.

The myth is partially true. You must ask yourself the question of what is changing rapidly—is it trends or events?

As Aesop illustrated in one his old and respected fables, every truth has two sides. What you see on television, hear on the radio, and read in the papers are events, and these change quickly. Events have always changed quickly no matter what time period you examine. You might say by definition events change quickly. On the other hand, economic trends change slowly but take on a life of their own. They move to an extreme and then reverse themselves. No trend lasts forever, but they can last for sometime.

An example of this is the very low saving rate of Americans. This has not always been the case. In the mid 1980's Americans save about 8% of their disposable income. As the great bull market in stocks roared on into the 1990's the saving rate declined precipitously to now where it is negative at times. This trend can not go on forever and will slowly begin to reverse itself. There will be consequences to this.

It will be your ability to adapt to the changing economic trends that will insure your success both personally and professionally. Why? Because if you do not base your planning on long-term economic trends, then it will be difficult to adopt a framework to base your financial and business decisions. You will be rushing about putting out current fires instead of devoting your energies to long-term planning. Then, what is the pivotal long-term economic/business trend that will significantly impact your planning?

The dominant economic trend now and well into the next decade will be a deflating price structure. There are a few reasons for this. One is the increase in competition due to the rapid spread of technology. This state-of-the-art productive technology allows the small entrepreneur to compete successfully with the large mega corporations. This more productive technology has also spread worldwide. Companies abroad, large or small, can now employ this latest technology to compete on the worldwide market for goods and services. When competition increases the pressure on prices is downward.

There are other forces at play that will put downward pressure on prices and hence companies profit margins. The saving rate in the United States is abysmally low. According to figures released by the U.S. Government, the combined saving rate for households in 2006 was a negative one-percent. This was the lowest since 1933. If you remember correctly, 1933 was the pit of the Great Depression. Households were not saving much then because twenty-five plus percent of the workforce was unemployed and had to live off of their savings.

This trend of very low to no saving at all will not continue. Think about it; there are only two things you can do with a dollar. You can either spend it or save it. As you start to save more in the margin, you spend less in percentage terms. Meanwhile the worldwide production of goods and services is still increasing at an increasing rate. So what happens to prices or the pressure on prices when production is still increasing and people are starting to save more? The pressure is on the downside.

There is another important force in play that will also put downward pressure on prices and hence the revenue or sales of businesses. The populations in the major western industrialized countries are aging. This is especially true in Europe and Japan, but also in the United States. Where do advertisers in print, on TV, and on the radio direct their advertising? It is primarily to the population age group between 18 to 40 years olds. As the population ages, they will tend to spend more on health care and vitamins, but less on other goods and services. Again, more downward pressure on prices and business profit margins.

As a businessperson or entrepreneur, coping in this type of environment will require that you devote more of your energies and capital in building market share even at the price of a little lower return-on-investment. On an individual or personal level, you should be focusing your attention on investments that are both liquid and safe. The important question to ask yourself is how easily is it to exit this investment if I wish? Avoid investments that are both illiquid and difficult to exit.

The old saying that cash is king is not completely true in this environment. The correct saying is that LIQUIDITY IS KING.

Myth #3:

The business cycle can be eliminated.

This myth is true—if you could remove humans from the face of the planet. Outside of this, the business cycle will always be here. It is part of the human psyche and behavior.

How does the business cycle arise? Some wise philosopher noted a long time ago that people can tolerate any condition except the possibility of one. They can endure war, famine, floods, pestilence, etc. and then go on with their lives. The one condition they have a hard time enduring though is <u>prolong periods of prosperity.</u> Incredulous as it sounds this observation contains more than just a kernel of truth. It is this one condition that gives rise to the business cycle.

When the economy starts to recover from a stiff downturn or business recession, people are understandably doubtful about the young expansion. They are very much risk averse and hold back on their discretionary spending and primarily their use of debt. As the upswing progresses, people become more tolerant of risk and especially the use of debt. Another way of stating it is that they become less risk averse or slightly greedier.

As the upturn ages, people forget the last downturn and become much more confident and think this expansion will last indefinitely. Businesses relax their guard and take on more debt to leverage their profit margins. Not to be left behind, the consumer will also be increasing their debt burdens to finance their growing consumption habit. The Federal Reserve (the FED) soon starts to worry about the escalating price pressures building in the economy and starts to raise interest rates. Soon a point is reached where the cost of servicing the debt is growing far faster than the incomes to pay both the principle and interest expenses. This is especially true for the consumer, which makes up 70% of the economy.

Now the expansion starts to stall because businesses and consumers can not sustain this credit expansion. A period of credit liquidation ensues and a new downturn begins. The severity of the new downturn depends on several factors. Besides the amount and cost of the credit or debt outstanding, these include the oversupply of goods and services and government economic polices such as tax and trade polices. What is more worrisome in this current expansion is that the consumer has little or no savings to fall back on during hard times. The consequence of this is that the next downturn or recession could be more severe than the garden type variety we had in the post World War ll era.

The business cycle will always be with us. Each cycle has a life of its own and varies in both amplitude and duration. Your goal as an individual or entrepreneur is to use the swings in the business cycle to enhance your value or the value or net worth of your business.

Myth #4:

The purpose of any investment is to make money.

It goes without saying that when you first read this myth there can be no doubt that the myth is true. Everyone knows that the purpose of any investment is to make money—right? Isn't that the reason why individuals buy stocks, bonds, real estate, and other investments? Also, I might add by using significant amount of borrowed money (leverage).

If you, both as individuals and business people, think short-term then this myth is true and correct and there is no need to read any further. Venture on to the next myth. But, if you wish to orient your planning based on long-term trends, then this common axiom of investing is flawed. It is probably more than flawed; it simply isn't true.

In today's economic environment the strategic groundrule that must govern your investment strategy is—the PURPOSE of any investment is not to make money but to increase your NET WORTH. This net worth may be on a personal level or it can be the net worth of your business. Another way of thinking about net worth is to substitute the word "value". In the business marketplace you want to increase the value of your business to your stockholders or maybe to a buyout firm. As individuals, you are exploring ways to increase your value as a person.

There is an important psychological benefit in focusing on increasing your net worth vs. just making money. It forces you to expand your time horizons and think long-term instead of short-term quick fixes. In other words it forces you to ask the question of what actions or steps can I take today that will increase the value or net worth of my business five to ten years down the road. The same applies to you as an individual. Isn't this why you learn a trade or profession? The danger in short-term investment thinking is that investments are made on the spur of the moment without regard to any specific plan or long-term consequences.

Thinking in terms of "making money" has a tendency of shifting or focusing your business energies towards the quarterly bottom line. In the highly competitive business environment we are in and with downward pressure on prices, increasing the top line (sales or revenues) will be of paramount importance. Think of the revenues of your business as the potential energy of the enterprise. As you increase your revenues, you raise the potential energy of the firm. Hence, you increase the value (net worth) of the business.

W. C. Fields noted that any dead fish can float downstream, but it takes a live one to swim upstream. Those individuals that are willing to take the longer-term perspective and focus on increasing their net worth will flourish in what will be a turbulent business economy.

Myth #5:

Rate-of-return is the most important investment criterion.

We all make investments whether as individuals or businesspersons. Therefore, with the maze of investment choices available what yardstick would be the most appropriate for both individuals and businesspeople to gauge each one? Some people make their investment decisions based primarily on rate-of-return, while others deem safety of paramount importance. Some others focus on the tax aspects of an investment.

While all of these concerns are important, they should not be deciding factor in basing your investment decisions. The most important investment criterion is the <u>suitability</u> of an investment in relation to your financial psychology. For the businessperson it simply means don't invest in a business you know nothing about. It is foolish to make a capital expenditure that does not have the potential to significantly increase your sales and add to your bottom line.

A business example that illustrates the role of investment suitability is the misadventure of Pacific Enterprises Corp. In the 1980's Pacific Enterprises, a large gas utility holding company in southern California, bought the retail drug chain Thrifty Drug Corp. (now part of Rite Aid). The company thought they could easily transfer their expertise of managing a utility over to the retail drug business. Bad decision! They overpaid for the retail drug chain by issuing a large amount of corporate debt. In addition, they knew nothing about the unique problems of managing a retail drug establishment. They simply got too far afield from their core business. Their losses started to grow and the company's stock value plummeted. Pacific Enterprises was forced to sell Thrifty Drug Corp. at a sizable loss. The investment they made in Thrifty was not a suitable one when compared to their core business.

Another way of looking at suitability is that it is the nexus between business risk and maximizing your rate-of-return. If you are in the business world you have to accept risk. Business is risk. There is a difference, though, of shooting for the moon and taking a calculated risk. The financial debacles of both Enron and Global Crossing illustrate an important point. Both companies decided to utilize large amounts of leverage (debt) to quickly expand both their top and bottom lines. In their conceit they forgot one important rule when utilizing debt. Even the ancient Persians know that LEVERAGE IS A TWO-EDGED SWORD. When business conditions are in your favor, leverage can rapidly expand both your top and bottom lines.

Turbulence and chaos characterize market economies. They are not well behaved organisms. In other words they are not linear. They are not predictable. Most likely, it is not a question of will the business environment change to adversely impact your original plans but when. When this happens, reverse leverage can cut you to ribbons.

The bankruptcies of Enron and Global Crossing plus the difficulties Tyco International encountered all were based on what I call corporate swagger. Assuming an optimistic business scenario, they all took on an enormous amount of debt to expand their businesses rapidly. Due to their overconfidence, they did not ask the suitable question when they were ballooning their debt to equity ratios. This question is—if the market conditions change (they will) can we **manage** the burden of this debt without hitting the ropes and going down. If this question was initially asked, they and many others could have saved their stockholders and employees much grief.

Therefore, for the businessperson, you have to ask the question when financing your plans should I use debt or equity? Debt is more risky, but it allows for faster growth. Equity financing is not as risky and hence allows for more stable growth. Without asking yourself the question as to whether this particular financing method and its risks and rewards are suitable to my operation, you may make reckless business decisions that do not mesh with sound financial management and your basic business philosophy.

You must decide the level of risk that is suitable for your comfort level on both a personal and professional level. Important Rule—the higher the rate-of-return the greater the risk of losing your money. There is no such thing as a free lunch.

Rate-of-return, though, is important in that it can be used to gauge the suitability of an investment. Before committing to any investment, it is important to realistically quantify the potential annual rate-of-return. This number will give you a relative "feel" of the level of risk involved.

To gauge this level of investment risk, take the interest rate on 10 year U.S. Treasury notes and add three to four percentage points to it. Rates-of-return that are equal or exceed this range are deemed risky investments. For example, the current interest rate on ten year Treasury notes is about 4.7%. Therefore, investments that may have a return in excess of 8% carry a higher potential risk. These investments may or may not be suitable for you.

Myth #6:

Raising taxes has no impact on interest rates.

This myth can also be stated as what impact will increasing taxes have on the level of interest rates? This is important because we live and work in a credit society, and a credit society implies an economy driven by debt or leverage. The myth actually has added importance considering that the current business expansion has resulted primarily by consumers whittling away their savings and borrowing against their homes and using their credit cards. There is no cushion or buffer in the economy.

With Congress in the habit of spending more than it takes in, it is not a big leap in imagination to assume they will eventually raise taxes. It really doesn't matter if the controlling party is the Democrats or the Republicans. Politicians will, like electrons in a circuit, take the path of least resistance. This path will be to raise taxes. Therefore, if increasing taxes (income taxes for example) impacts the level of interest rates, this will have a direct bearing on our ability as individuals and as a nation to service our massive debt build-up.

As stated in the introduction, economics is the study of human behavior in its historical setting. Therefore, human nature being what it is, people will always try to maintain their existing standard-of-living in the face of adversity. If an individual's or family's disposal income is reduced by raising taxes, then in order to maintain their current living standard, people will tend to reduce the amount they save. The extra amount induced by the increased taxes comes out of savings. The net effect of raising taxes is that the national level of savings is lowered even further from our already abysmally low rate. To induce the needed funds to help finance the explosive growth of debt, interest rates will have to rise in real terms (after inflation is stripped away).

Instead of having no effect on interest rates, raising taxes on a national level can have the perverse effect of increasing the level of real interest rates. Since we are a high consumption—low saving country, we would have to draw in more money from foreign investors to finance our debt. Like most rational people, they would like to be compensated for the increase risks of holding more of our debt. The result—increase upward pressure on rates and a drag on further economic expansion.

There is another perverse impact on raising taxes especially on upper income earners. It has to do with class warfare and the destruction of opportunity. When you increase the taxes on the well off, especially entrepreneurs, you are taxing away more than their monies or capital. You are also taxing away their opportunities to create wealth. And here is the irony—when you tax away opportunity from those who have made it, do you not also tax away opportunities from those who wish to make it? There is a linkage in our society. Taxing away opportunities from those who have done well will also destroy opportunities for the rest of society.

This myth exposes many of the ironies of political policy. Bad economic policy, even for the best of reasons, is still bad policy. We all pay the price.

Myth #7:

In our current business environment liquidity is not important.

Remember the saying from one of Clint Eastwood's <u>Dirty Harry</u> movies—"A man has got to know his limitations". This applies equally well to the art of economic forecasting. The art (not science) of economics is useful in forecasting what the predominant risks are facing our national economy and the resulting consequences. It is not sufficient to say that next year our business economy will grow at a 3% rate and inflation will be 2%. This is sheer crystal ball gazing and not of much use. With this in mind let's examine our national economy and see why liquidity, both on a professional and personal level, will be king for the next decade at least.

Do you have a metal chain in your house? Take a look at it. You will notice all the links are of equal size. The U.S. economy can, in a way, be represented by the links in a chain. But, the difference is that the economic links are not of equal size. In addition, some links are weaker than others.

The biggest link in our national economic chain is the consumer or more explicitly consumption expenditures. This link now represents 70% of our Gross Domestic Product (GDP) and dwarfs all the other economic links combined. This link is also the weakest link in our chain and is the one of most concern.

To put it succinctly, the consumer is tapped-out. With the direction of interest rates trending higher, Americans can not continue spending money they do not have. Household borrowing is increasing substantially faster than incomes. Even though real wages are increasing, most of the increase is being absorbed by substantially higher medical insurance premiums. We use to talk about a healthy savings rate in this country. Now, we have little to none. The most important link in our economic chain is extremely illiquid. This will have long-term consequences for economic growth and, hence, the ability of companies to maintain their profitability and grow their top-line. Eventually consumers will have to rebuild their balance sheets and save more and spend less in the margin.

There are some things worse than having a recession—having none at all. Recessions provide the impetus for both consumers and businesses to rebuild their liquidity. It is a painful process, but it sets the stage for the next strong upward expansion. For example, in the early 1990 recession the average American household **pared** their debt by an inflation adjusted $410. This helped set the stage for the strong expansion in the 1990's. In the 2001 recession, the average U.S. household **added** $1,420 to their debt levels.

It is possible for awhile to avoid a business recession through the Federal Reserve policy of manipulating interest rates. But, the price to be paid is high. The economy can flounder along in a tepid sluggish manner and can easily stumble into a more serious recession. You are sort of operating in an economic Twilight Zone between growth and stagnation.

Another consideration is the unusual political alliance in Washington. Democrats and Republicans in Congress disagree on many political matters, but there is one fundamental economic point they do agree on. They both like to spend increasing amounts of money on programs that can't be sustained. Eventually tax rates will go up no matter who is in the White House.

This is unfortunate because large cuts in marginal tax rates is the one thing that can produce both sustained and substantial increases in economic growth. In the 1920's then Secretary of the Treasury Mellon went through an exhaustive study to determine what top incremental tax rate would maximize income to government yet, also, provide meaningful incentives for individuals to take business risks. The answer was a top rate of 25%. This is far lower than the current top rate of 35%. In addition there were no phase-outs of deductions then based on income levels. For example, in 2007 for married couples filing jointly, there is a phase out of itemized deductions at an adjusted gross income starting at $156,400. The net effect is to increase the marginal tax rate above the nominal value.

The question, then, is how do you grow your business in an environment that will be highly competitive and turbulent? The most logical answer is to increase prices of the goods and services your company offers. Logical—yes, but it is not realistic. If anything, with the economic environment described above, the market will be dictating downward pressure on prices—not upside. This leaves one other alternative—going after **market share**.

We have had the mistaken belief in this country that the business future belongs to the big and the mighty. This is not true. The future belongs to the **swift**. The swift are those men and women whose businesses have liquidity (low debt levels) and are generating sufficient levels of free cash flow to take advantage of opportunities that will be presenting themselves. Free cash flow is the wherewithal, the stuff, that successful business people can use to innovate new products and services, which along with effective marketing and customer relations can be used to grab market share from your competitors.

Additionally, those businesses that have liquidity and cash flow can also secure market share by lowering prices while still maintaining profitability. This line of survival thinking falls under the category of guerrilla marketing. Let's face it—it is a jungle out there, and the swift and nimble are the ones who will prosper in this environment.

People tend to make situations more complex than they are. This evolves from a tendency in human nature to drift from the simple to the complex. But, in business it does not have to be this way. If you can focus on building-up the free cash flow in your business (and it wouldn't hurt your personal life either), you will both increase its value and have a competitive edge in the marketplace. It is that simple.

Myth #8:

The Federal Reserve controls interest rates.

What interest rates are we talking about and why is it important to the economy and to individuals?

There is an old saying that money makes the world go around. In economic parlance this is not quite correct. Actually, it is the cost of money that makes the world go around, and the cost of money is reflected in the level of interest rates. As the level of interest rates rise, businessmen and investors demand a higher rate of return on their capital investment to justify the expenditure. The result is similar to "walking up a pyramid"—fewer and fewer capital expenditures will justify the targeted rate of return. As productive investment decreases, so does the speed at which money changes hands (velocity of money). With some time lag the economy slows and unemployment starts to increase.

With such importance attached to interest rates, does the Federal Reserve Board (FED) really control their level? To simplify, we must differentiate between short term and long term rates. Interest rates on securities that mature in a year or less would be considered short term, while interest rates on securities that mature in ten years or more would denote long term rates.

The myth is true in that the FED does have a powerful impact on short term interest rates, namely the federal funds rate and its brother, the three month U.S. Treasury bill rate. The federal funds rate is an overnight rate at which banks lend to each other. The FED controls short term rates by adding or subtracting reserves from the banking system. By adding reserves, they tend to put downward pressure on short term rates and by subtracting reserves they do the opposite.

Long term interest rates, though, are set more by the market than by the FED. These rates reflect peoples' expectations of economic growth, inflation, and how much foreigners are willing to lend us to meet our investment needs. As stated before, since we are a high consumption and a low saving country, how much foreigners are willing to lend us has an over-sized impact on long term rates.

Why are interest rates important? When a business issues a 10 year bond yielding 8%, then that business is assuming they can profitably invest the funds in an enterprise earning a much better return than 8%. If this weren't so, why would anyone want to take the risks of potential bankruptcy and issue a bond?

What is important is not the level of short term or long term interest rates, but the spread between them. As the FED tightens up on the money supply (by subtracting reserves from the banking system), short term rates will climb faster than long term rates. If short term interest rates should climb above long term rates, this historically is an early warning sign that economy will be slowing significantly—possibly entering a business recession. When short term rates are above long term rates, this is called an inverted yield curve. You would rationally expect short term rates to be below long term rates because of the extra risks of holding a longer term bond.

When this happens, it would be best to rebuild your working capital by reducing your short term debt levels. One way to accomplish this is to move your shorter term debt (a year or less) into a longer term bond (say 10 years or more) if possible. The net effect is to rebuild your liquidity.

When the business economy starts to slow significantly, liquidity will be king.

Myth #9:

The rules of economics are too complicated.

This myth is true only if you believe it. In reality, the rules or laws of economics can be boiled down to a few concise premises. Listening to all the talking heads or political pundits on television or the radio will only leave one confused and disjointed.

I have listed below, what I call the four simple laws of economics. If you can understand these, it will eliminate much of the confusion that emanates from the popular press.

These four laws are:

1. There is no such thing as a free lunch. There is always a "price" which has to be paid by someone. This rule is of paramount importance.

2. The markets are the masters—price controls <u>do not</u> work. You can not simultaneously control both the price and quantity of anything. If you control the price of anything, the supply of that good or service will go down.

3. Economic events do not exist in isolation. We do not live and work in an economic vacuum.

4.   Economics and politics are inseparable. Two choices:

   a.   Policies that lead to real income growth

   b.   Policies that lead to redistribution of income.

   c.   NOTE: There is a _price_ to be paid for both a & b above.

Rule number four is important. In number 4b the policies that lead to a redistribution of income are usually associated with raising taxes on the so called well to do or the rich. You can read this another way and say taxes will be raised on the more creative members of our society or the entrepreneur class. When you tax away creative capital from the entrepreneur class, the price to be paid is a loss of vibrancy in the economy. Employment opportunities start to fade along with economic growth. This says nothing about the loss of tax revenue to both the Federal and state governments.

To be fair, what is the price to be paid by number 4a? One price is a more vibrant and opportunistic marketplace. What this means is that more businesses will be created and entering the market with their respective products and services. It will be a highly competitive marketplace characterized by growth, turbulence, and insecurity. But, this is what market economies are all about. The future does not belong to the big or the small but to the **swift.** The swift will be those who have the wherewithal to take advantage of the exploding opportunities.

Myth #10:

In life attitude is everything.

First, why would someone who writes and speaks predominately on business and economic trends write on this particular subject? Isn't this somewhat out-of-character with the theme of the book?

If you use the modern definition of economics, i.e., "the science that deals with the production, distribution, and consumption of commodities", then you would have a valid point. But, as I stated before, if we use the classical definition of economics—**"the study of human behavior in its historical setting"**—the theme of the myth meshes with the purpose of the book.

As both economic and political mortals, we live and work in an environment that is in constant motion or movement. This movement is, by its nature, turbulent. There are a few consequences of this.

The first is that turbulent motion has no predictability. In other words, you do not know where it is going or what the results will be. A good example of this would be the stock market. How many "experts" eventually end up with "egg on their face"? Therefore, in the business of life do not make any detailed plans. Plan only in broad strokes and even then your plans will shift and change. The old saying that when man plans,

God laughs is still true. The second consequence is more oriented towards this article.

If both our economic environment and we are in constant motion (turbulent), how could you always maintain a positive attitude, or as the popular literature states, a PMA (positive mental attitude)? You simply can't. Mortals are not designed that way. Your attitude, like our environment, is always in motion. Then, if attitude is not the most important criterion of success and advancement, what is?

The primary criterion that separates success from failure is action, namely **positive action**. Your attitude or state-of-mind can be in the gutter. So what! Nothing stays the same forever.

What do I mean by positive action? Or, to put it another way, what positive actions should you take. You take the necessary actions today that will increase the net worth or value of your investment (business, etc.) tomorrow. From a business perspective, though, there is an important point to consider. In this highly competitive and turbulent economy, building the value of your business can be achieved by focusing on increasing the free cash flow of your enterprise. Free cash flow is the real money after all expenses that can be returned to the owners of the business. The value of a business is a direct function of its free cash flow. By building the cash flow of the business, you now have the resources—the stuff—to take advantage of opportunities that will present themselves.

On an individual level, it means taking the necessary actions to learn a set of skills that would be hard to transfer to an individual overseas working for less money. It could mean going to college to learn a profession or a trade, i.e., plumber, carpenter, electrician, computer repair, etc. It also means watching your debt levels and don't get over leveraged to the point where you need every paycheck just to stay in place. Start a savings plan like a 401K, Roth IRA, or even a traditional IRA and contribute to it yearly. By doing so, the eighth wonder of the world will kick in. This is the law of compound interest.

Famous Amos, the chocolate chip cookie king, had two words to express his business philosophy. These two words are "**Do It**". Taking the necessary actions to build the value of your investment will always be of paramount importance. Good fortune favors the bold. Attitude follows action.

Myth #11:

Personal investing is a tricky and complicated affair.

There is some validity to this myth in that people who have complex estates and business ventures need some type of investment and/or legal advice. This can be achieved through the use of a professional tax accountant or lawyer specializing in this trade. For the average John and Jane Doe, it is true only to the extent you are willing to buy into it. Financial planners and similar types have it in their best interests to make it seem like personal investing is complex and beyond your abilities.

With your money or capital there are only two generic investments you can make. They are 1. The financial investments, and 2. The tangible or commodity investments. An example of the first would be stocks and bonds (the so called paper investments). The second includes a myriad of investments, such as, oil, gold, grains, pork bellies, coffee, and etc. Real estate, being very popular until recently, would also fall into this second category.

With the rise of exchange trades funds (ETF), it is now possible to combine both of these generic types of investments. ETF are very similar to mutual funds, but differ in that they are traded just like ordinary stocks. For example, there are ETF funds that specialize in gold, U.S. oil and gas, real estate, and etc. You can also buy an ETF that are composed of stocks in the financial sector, foreign stock markets and the utility sectors. You name the area of interest and you can probably find an ETF that specializes in it.

Before investing in any particular area, it is important to ask yourself the question—what type of investment is suitable for me? As stated in a previous myth, **suitability** is the most important investment criterion. For example, up till very recently owning and renting real estate has been a red hot area to invest in. But, if you don't like dealing with all the problems that investing in real estate entails like problems with noisy tenants including evictions (which can take a few months), being called up in the middle of the night to fix a toilet or other plumbing problems, maybe you should forgo direct ownership. If still interested in real estate, examine the possibility of owning a REIT (real estate investment trust). Again, these trade just like stocks and usually pay a good dividend. They also specialize. Some own just residential apartments throughout the country while others invest in commercial non-residential properties. These would include shopping centers and office buildings. More information on REITs can be found at your local library. The Value Line Investment Survey, found usually at the reference desk of the library, has information on numerous REITs. It is also a good source to evaluate individual stocks.

Lastly, I will deal with one other very important point that is pertinent to all investments and that is how do I get out of it? Is it easy to sell? Real estate, by definition, is an illiquid investment. If liquidity is important to you (and it should be), then think twice before jumping into the real estate market.

This now brings us to the stock market and owning stocks in good quality companies. Since 1920, stocks on average have returned nine to ten percent per year including dividends. There have some years where they have plummeted down and others where they have zoomed up. Stocks, just like owning your own business, are risky. Good quality ones, though, are liquid. You can buy or sell these in the touch of a keystroke on your computer. But, remember this, even good quality stocks in a down market (bear market) will go down.

If interested in the market, but don't know what stocks to buy, why not buy the Dow Jones Industrials or the stocks in the S&P 500 index through an exchange trade fund. The exchange trade fund called the Diamonds (symbol DIA) represents all the stocks composing the Dow Jones Industrial Average while the exchange traded fund called the SPDR 500 (symbol SPY) represents the stocks composing the Standard & Poor's 500 index. Both of these ETF move in tandem with their respective index. With them you own a fractional share of every stock composing either the Dow Jones Industrials or the S&P 500 indexes. These two ETF take the thinking out of which stock to own. Don't forget that if either or both of these two indexes should go down both the DIA and the SPY will follow. Both of these ETF are very liquid.

Now let us take this a little bit further. This paragraph is for those individuals who find writing covered call options suitable for part of their investment strategy. Both the DIA and the SPY exchange traded funds have call options on them. This gives the owner of the call option the right (but not the obligation) to buy the respective ETF at a certain price within a certain time limit. Let's do an example. Say you buy 100 shares of the DIA. At the current price (the price fluctuates with the market) that would be $12,777 plus commissions. At current prices you can sell someone the right, call option, to buy your 100 DIA shares at $13,200 between now and seven months out for approximately $340 minus commissions. This $340 is yours to keep no matter what. If at the time of expiration of the call option the price should be below $132 per share, the option will expire worthless and you can write or sell another one. If it is above $132 per share, your 100 shares of DIA will be called away from you. Don't get greedy. If it is called away from you, you have already made your money. Your one hundred shares of DIA has gone from approximately $128 per share to $132. In addition you received $340 minus commissions in option premium.

The above investment strategy is not for everyone. The type of investor that it may appeal to is the more active one. The "buy it and forget it" type of investor should stay away from this strategy. For those who do wish to pursue this type of strategy (covered call writing), I strongly recommend using a discount brokerage firm. Full service brokers charge way too much in commissions. The more you save in commissions the more money in your pocket and the less in theirs.

A final word about stock brokers working at full service firms. We all have our biases including me. You might say especially me. If at all possible, I would recommend you avoid stockbrokers at full service firms. They work for the firm not for you. Their goal is to sell you products that will generate fee or commission income for both them and the firm. Whether these products are suitable for you is of secondary or tertiary importance to them. Recent history has shown that this is more often the case. To say that Wall Street has cleaned itself up is laughable. Please think of full service stockbrokers <u>as used car salesmen in fancy suits</u>.

I will conclude this myth by writing about pure unadulterated safety. Did you ever hear of the food pyramid? There is also an investment pyramid. It works this way. The bottom of the pyramid, the base, should form the safest part of your investment portfolio. Another way of stating it would be that the base should be the least risky of your investments. As you move up the pyramid, your investments become more and more risky with the potential of larger rates of return. The amount of risk you wish to take is totally up to you (suitability). Realize this, though, the larger the potential rate of return the increasing likelihood you have of losing your money.

In constructing your base and in my opinion, the safest investments on this planet are short term obligations of the U.S. Government—namely three month or six month Treasury Bills. You will always be repaid even if the Treasury has to print the money. Name one other safe investment that can say that? In addition the interest earned on U.S. Treasury Securities is state income tax free—not Federal. This might be important to individuals living in high income tax states.

How do you purchase U.S. Treasury Bills? You buy them directly from the U.S. Treasury by opening-up a Legacy Treasury Direct Account. There is no commission or fee when purchasing Treasury Bills directly from the U.S. Treasury. Do not purchase them from a bank or brokerage house. They will charge you a commission or fee for their services. Once you have a Legacy Treasury Direct Account number, you can purchase them directly over a touch tone phone.

The steps in establishing a Legacy Treasury Direct Account are listed below.

Steps

- First call the U. S. Treasury at (800) 722-2678 and order the form for opening a Legacy Treasury Direct account. To speak to a representative, press key #5 or just stay on the phone.

- The info you will need to complete the form

  1. The name on the account

2. Your checking account # and the nine digit bank routing number, name of bank, phone # of bank

3. The address of the person on the account

4. The social security number of the person on the account

5. Sign the form and return to Treasury. They will then issue you an account number.

- T-Bills are bought in multiples of $1,000.00.

Myth #12:

We are entering a new feudal society with new lords and serfs. Or—how to prosper in the coming age of poverty and privilege.

There is an old saying that goes something like this—what goes around comes around. This saying is plausible, but not entirely correct. What goes around does come around, but in a different shape and form. To more fully appreciate this new "feudal society" we will be entering, we must first examine where we have been and the consequences flowing from that time and place.

The period from about 1995 to 2000 was a very unique interval in our economic/business history. The economic events that occurred in this time period happen at most twice in a century. This period of time is called a founder's economy, and the years 1995 to 2000 comprised the first stage of this founders economy. It is a time of fundamental and rapid technological and economic transformation of society. The transformation is permanent, and it seems to defy the laws of economic gravity. The last such period occurred in the 1920's. This resulted from the confluence of the rapid electrification of the U.S. along with the mass introduction of the automobile.

The first stage of a founder's economy ends in a bubble and it does pop. When it does, the second stage is called the "blood in the streets" phase. We are in that phase now and it will dictate our new social and economic environment.

The term "blood in the streets" does not necessarily imply actual corporal fighting. Instead the term means an intense period of business competition. This second stage can easily last 15 to 20 years. It continues until the weak business enterprises are filtered out. The difference now, compared to the previous founder's economy, is that not only do you have intense business competition within our national borders but also internationally. The Internet, along with inexpensive communication and transportation costs, has helped to transform the international marketplace. In this second phase, how companies compete and price their goods and services will give rise to the new business serfs and lords—*the new feudal society*.

From the end of World War II till the late 1990's companies more often than not used the cost-driven model to price their product or service. In this model a company added up all their costs to produce a product or service and then tacked-on a competitive profit margin. This, then, determined the price at which to sell their product or service. For the majority of times it worked.

It is in this second stage of intense business competition that the traditional cost driven model breaks down. Competition is intense because dramatic worldwide increases in productivity have led to too many goods chasing too little demand. Companies now have very little pricing power.

Companies now have to use a price driven model of pricing. This model answers the question: what price will cause my firm's product or service to clear the market. In other words, what price will give me a competitive advantage? It is usually a lower price than the cost driven price, but with that comes less competition.

Once you determine the price of your product or service with the price driven model, you do everything in your power to slash all costs. This includes labor, medical, inventory, material, and any other expense than can be cut. No cost is sacred. In this second phase you have to reduce all expenses to stay competitive.

It is this second phase of the founder's economy that will give rise to the new business "lords" and "serfs". The new lords will be those business people who can quickly discern, adapt to, and exploit the unpredictable movement in the turbulent flow of life. The new lords will be those business people that have as their target the goal of growing the **free cash flow** of their business. This cash flow represents the means—the wherewithal—for those shrewd business people to take advantage of opportunities and events that present themselves. By so growing the free cash flow of a business not only do you increase its value, but also you provide it with the means to maintain its market share and possibly increase it. On the other hand, the new serfs are those businesses that are mired in debt and illiquidity. If they stay this way, they will travel down the road to extinction.

I direct major emphasis on building free cash flow primarily because you could be the smartest business manager alive but without the free cash flow (the financial means); it will be difficult to capitalize on opportunities in this second phase. Having an ample free cash flow allows you the opportunity to take business risks and survive the possibility of failure. It also allows you to hire the talent necessary to grow your business and expand your market share.

In the old feudal society (circa 1200 AD), everything was rather constant. If you were born a serf, that is where you stayed. If you were born a lord, that is where you belonged. In the new feudal society nothing is constant. Through luck, change of management focus, and acquisitions it is very possible that business serfs can become lords. Conversely, if business lords should lose their focus and become complacent in this extremely competitive phase, they could stumble down the path toward serfdom.

Lastly, one must keep in mind that the novel conditions with which businesses now have to deal to remain viable entities in the coming decades will have a seismic impact on the social order and the expectations prevailing among the individuals who make it up. The future belongs to those individuals (lords) that have the intellectual acumen to anticipate and the wherewithal and flexibility to take advantage of developing opportunities. The serfs are maladroit and floundering in debt. It will be difficult for them to seize opportunities.

The second phase of the founder's economy will be more turbulent than that which preceded it. But, therein lie the opportunities for those who can and wish to be lords. Out of turbulence comes the potential for growth.

To paraphrase Mel Brooks—**it is good to be a business lord.**

Myth #13:

Government is your friend—the conservation of personal power.

For the purpose of this myth I am more concerned with governmental power on the Federal level than on the state or local levels. Although, with the immense growth of states' spending and new programs, the myth also applies to them. The myth may have a sliver of truth, but dangerous in any event.

With the rise of the welfare state, especially after World War II, it was commonly believed (and still is) that government can be a friend or ally in promoting the well being of some sectors of the economy. Thus, talk of an economic partnership between government, business, and labor was quite common. There is no argument that government can be of assistance in promoting the well being of society. There are many government programs (maybe not run the most efficiently) that can attest to this. The problem arises that in this relationship between government and the private sector, it is assumed the relationship will be equal.

Even though in the post World War II political economy these programs did have and do have some beneficial results on the betterment of society, there are some unintentional side effects. One of the unintentional side effects is that government has increased its influence and power in the economy. In ways this had been good in that it has corrected some abuses in our society. A few that come to mind are discrimination laws against voting and employment.

Like the conservation of matter in physics, there is a conservation of personal power that applies to the relationship of the individual to government. The conservation of matter states that matter can not be created or destroyed except by extraordinary means (nuclear fusion or fission for example). The conservation of personal power (political and economic) simply states that power can not be created or destroyed, but it can be transferred.

The tools of power have changed throughout the ages, but the amount of government's economic and political power has been relatively constant. You can not empower the individual to have more power or control over their destinies and also empower the government to provide more opportunities. Someone or some group has to pay a price. The price is a loss of empowerment and eventually a loss of freedom.

Let's put this into a different perspective. In one of my other "myths", I stated the four simple laws of economics. In one of these I said that you could not control both the price and quantity of anything. In a similar vein, if you wish for government to provide more economic security and still wish to have an expanding set of economic and political freedoms, you are wishing for something that has never been or will be. The conservation of power says you must give up something to receive a special benefit.

The consequences of this can have a chilling impact in the marketplace. When businesses and trade groups petition and receive special favors from Congress and the administration, they will benefit initially. In doing so, they have transferred some of their freedom and flexibility to government bureaucrats.

The economic landscape is in a constant state of flux (turbulence would be a better word). What benefit that helps a particular group now will have a detrimental impact on other segments of our economic society.

An example—when President Bush, in his first term, imposed tariffs on imported steel it did help the U.S. steel industry and its employees. But, it had the negative consequence of driving up steel prices in the U.S. The effect was to drive up the cost of items manufactured from steel. Many of these manufactured items faced strong international competition in the marketplace. U.S. manufactured items became less competitive and employment outside the steel industry suffered. What jobs were saved in the U.S. steel industry were lost in other industries.

The conclusion-government is not necessarily your friend.

Conclusion:

The objective of political and economic systems

The introduction stated that economics is the study of human behavior in its historical setting. Consequently, it is the study of people; it is the study of psychology.

Individuals without a goal are like a piece of wood floating in the sea being moved aimlessly by the currents. They have no direction. Similarly, a political and economic system without a goal is also adrift and can move in ways that maybe harmful long term to the society. Stating it differently, when individuals lose their vision or focus of the future they tend to think short term instead of asking what actions can I take today that will increase my value or net worth over the longer haul. What applies to individuals also applies to societies.

In democratic societies all economic policies and priorities are realized through the political process. This then begs the question what should be the North Star of economic policy? The **economic objective** of political policy is to give individuals the incentives and opportunities to grow and prosper within the Rule of Law and the bounds of morality. Anything other than this will slowly eat away at the fabric of freedom and opportunity in American society.

How is this objective accomplished? It is accomplished by keeping the taxes on wealth creation as low as possible without the feeling that accumulated wealth is being confiscated by the government. In addition the monetary environment should provide for a stable currency. If wealth providers (entrepreneurs) feel that the national currency will be stable over a prolong period of time, it gives them the incentives to base their plans on a longer time horizon. Lastly, there must be a legal system in place honoring the law of contracts.

The above must seem like economic theory, but there is a nuts and bolts to it—namely employment opportunities. Over the last ten years seventy-five percent of the net new jobs created in the U.S. came from companies with 200 or less employees. The bigger more familiar companies are downsizing and laying off employees. For example, just look what is happening to employment at the big three U.S. auto companies. New business creation will be the locus of future wealth creation in the United States. This must be encouraged!

Lastly, let us talk about body surfing and the future—yours in particular. Have you ever tried bodysurfing? Bodysurfing is similar to hardboard surfing with the exception that your body is the board. The goal is to try to catch the wave as it starts to turn over and ride it until it breaks up or breaks you up.

For those of you who have tried it, maybe you noticed one very important characteristic. You can go further riding a small wave that is building momentum than riding the crest of a large one. In both your personal and business lives too many people are riding the crest of a larger wave. This is herd mentality. You have to find a wave that is building momentum and ride it. This will insure that you stay ahead of the herd. The tool that will help you accomplish this is to build liquidity (free cash flow in your business) in your personal lives. Liquidity or free cash flow is the wherewithal, the means that will enable you to take advantage of opportunities that will present themselves. *This theme has been repeatedly emphasized throughout this book for the simple reason it is now of paramount importance. The herd is illiquid.*

The human condition is marked by turbulence. Turbulence has some rather negative connotations, but it also has a strong positive aspect. Out of turbulence come the opportunities for growth and advancement. Those who are nimble and liquid will have a leading edge over the herd. You will be an agile predator.

Good surfing and good hunting!

"The true wealth of a state
consists in the number of
its inhabitants, in their
toil and industry."
—Napoleon

978-0-595-43983-6
0-595-43983-7